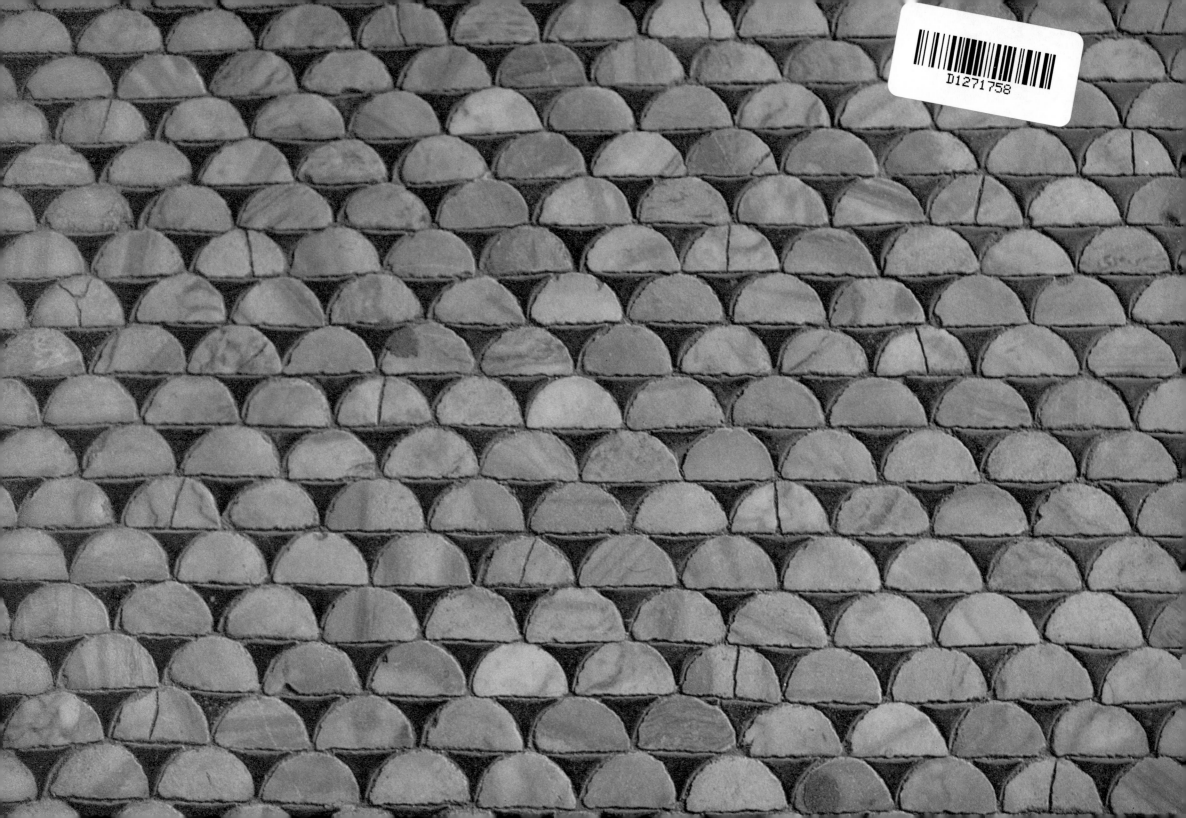

Venice

VENICE

Introduction by **Stephen Spender**

*with 182 photographs in full color
by* **Fulvio Roiter**

The Vendome Press
New York, Paris, Lausanne

Distributed by The Viking Press

Contents

Introduction

Venice is not just Venice. More than any other city of the past, except perhaps the Byzantium of the incandescent later poetry of Yeats, it has become transformed within the imaginations of artists, painters, poets, prose-writers. Yet unlike Byzantium degenerated into modern Istanbul, it remains very much as it was at the height of its greatest artistic achievements, during the Renaissance. We can set the Venice of the great Italian painters and of Turner's unique vision side by side against the living Venice of today and compare the two. Or have we been so influenced by the visions of genius that we cannot see the real place before us with our own eyes? The photographs in this volume should help us see how far the painters are justified in their transformation of Venice in their art, and also the literal nature of the real Venice we know today.

As early as 1882, Henry James observed that the most obvious thing to say about Venice is that there is nothing left to say. Venice preserved, the *Venice Observed* of Mary McCarthy's book (to which, together with Hugh Honour's *The Companion Guide to Venice*, I am indebted) has become transformed within the writings of Goethe, Heine, Byron, Shelley, Browning, Ruskin, de Nerval, Proust – to mention but a few names of writers which immediately spring to mind; and within the painting of Carpaccio, Giovanni Bellini, Titian,

Tintoretto – and indeed all Venetian painters. In the minds of the English their idea of Venice is probably still overlaid by half-remembered quotations from Ruskin and a few paintings of Turner which have transformed Venice into a special English Romantic vision.

Works of art associated with images of Venice tend to stick in my mind and evoke its atmosphere and architecture. After seeing Visconti's film *Death in Venice* (based on Thomas Mann's short story), whenever I hear the Adagietto of Mahler's Fifth Symphony which accompanies the photographed images of the Lagoon at dawn with which that film opens, I inevitably see a picture of the mouth of the Grand Canal with the island of San Giorgio Maggiore, and the domes of Sta Maria della Salute before me. And reading that Wagner wrote the second act of *Tristan* in Venice and that the melancholy tune played by the shepherd at the opening of the third act was suggested by the call of some gondolier at night along a dark canal, I will always see Venice in that music. Now, writing this, I remember how, after the first night of *The Rake's Progress*, people seated at tables in front of Florian's and other cafés in St Mark's Square, stood up and applauded Stravinsky as he walked past them, away from the theatre. The scene lives before my eyes.

Since the death of Stravinsky, the last of the magi, Venice is no longer the city of calm, toil, creation, luxury, that it was for artist-princes – Chopin, Liszt, Wagner, Gustav Mahler, Serge Diaghilev, whose work seems to fall from a banquet of their lives. Wagner regarded Venice as a good place in which to compose because you could see the crowds and yet be alone. Stravinsky – his friend and assistant Robert Craft tells us – loved the 'cosiness' of Venice. He also wished to be, and was, buried here.

Palaces, canals, gondolas, effects of light seen across the Lagoon at dawn and at sunset, dissolve into Romantic, fulgurous, sinister, poetic visions as in Shelley's lines which seem so close to Turner's visions of Venice:

> And the red tower looked gray, and all between
> The churches, ships and palaces were seen
> Huddled in gloom; – into the purple sea
> The orange hues of heaven sunk silently.
> We hardly spoke, and soon the gondola
> Conveyed me to my lodging by the way.

To Proust, years before he went there, Venice signified the fusion of the vision with the reality. He wrote in a review of a translation of Ruskin's *The Stones of Venice*:

The skin of Venice and the mosaics of St Mark's take on colours still more miraculous than their own, since they are the hues of a marvellous imagination, carried across the world, as in an enchanted ship, by Ruskin.

But his biographer, George Painter, informs us that when he went to Venice he was at first disappointed,

'because we cannot see things at once through the eyes of the body and the eyes of the mind' [Proust was] a bit disappointed to find the façade of St Mark's less like pearls and rubies than Ruskin had given him to expect. Next morning at ten o'clock, when his shutters were opened, his eyes were dazzled by the sunlight falling not, as usual, on the iron chimney-cowl of the next door house in Paris, but on the golden angel over the campanile of St Mark's, 'who brought me on his flashing wings a promise of beauty and joy greater than ever he bore to Christian hearts'.

But Venice, exceptionally capable though it be of transformation within the imaginations of men of genius, remains nonetheless obstinately, noisily, stinkingly, sordidly even, itself. A friend of mine told me how, going along a canal in a gondola, he noticed a drain-pipe affixed to a wall which was broken at the end, from which a turd dropped into the water. D. H. Lawrence called Venice 'An abhorrent, green, slippery city'. Many of today's Venetians would sympathize with him. Three years ago, when I was last there, a Venetian observed to my son, who was with me: 'We Venetians hate Venice. Only the tourists like it.' Doubtless many of them hate the houses for the unsalubrious dampness of the lower floors. Others hate living in a show-case.

Venice today, which most tourists notice as little as they would invisible spirits, is a fleshly, bustling, animated place, some of whose inhabitants are aristocrats who claim lineages going back to the late Roman Empire. The closest observers of Venice have been those who have known its dark canals as well as its stony light. The darkness sometimes comes to blot out the light for Venice-worshippers. This happened to Ruskin who turned against the city he had made enchantment in the mind of Proust. Hugh Honour quotes Ruskin: 'Through century after century of gathering vanity and fostering guile, that white dome of St Mark's had uttered into the ear of Venice "Know thou, that for all these things, God will bring thee into judgement".' And Browning saw the Venetians of history dancing their way towards the final decline 'when the kissing had to stop'.

Today the note of the nineteenth-century Old Testament prophet sounds a bit absurd, yet does it not awake a faint response in us? Throughout its history, we feel, Venice has disobeyed the Biblical injunction not to build your house on sand. And even if the barren islands at the top of the Adriatic to which the Roman refugees from the Barbarian invaders fled, has some very solid mud a few feet down into which millions of wooden piles could be effectively driven, nevertheless Venice's whole empire seems built on sand. Its survival into our own age after its long decline ending at last with the fall of the Republic is miraculous and yet resembles a long drawn out death-bed scene. Today when warnings of its imminent submersion ring louder than ever, we ask ourselves whether the disappearance of Venice would be the reward for a sinful past or whether it would not much rather be our punishment for our world of industrialism and pollution which has disturbed the tides and set up waves from motor-boats in the canals. If Venice disappeared we might feel that this was because we moderns were not worthy of this bright emanation of its age, as beautiful and frail and poignant as Botticelli's Venus standing upon her frilly shell among the bird-winged waves. Venice has always been inseparable from the shadow of her own fall, of which there have been, from time to time, singular warnings. This city that embodies, more than any other, the audacity and frailty of human history has yet survived less time-damaged than any other. One feels that for her finally to collapse would be a judgement of civilization more recent than her own.

A. J. A. Symons, in a letter to Edmund Gosse, summed up the Venice which he saw in 1890 and which seems not so greatly different from that of today:

> I cannot describe the curious mosaic of this Venetian existence. It is a jumble of palaces and post-houses, princesses and countesses, gondoliers and porters, hours and hours by day upon the lagoon, hours and hours by night in strange places of the most varied description.

Baron Corvo in his writings filled out the varieties of strange places.

The photographs in this volume do not explore very deeply the dark interior life of the Venice of back streets and the little canals in which, as Proust wrote, the visitor 'seems to penetrate further and further into the depths of some secret thing'. They do however present aspects of Venice which we can relate to each other and out of which we can construct a whole complex picture. One of these is the atmospheric Venice of the Lagoon and Grand Canal from which Turner's and Shelley's visions derive. Another is the near-coincidence of the camera's exact account of the palaces of the Grand Canal with some paintings of Canaletto. The photograph (88) of a part of the Grand Canal taken from the Rialto Bridge, with the view of the thirteenth-century Ca' da Mosto, looks as though it might have been painted by this artist. Photographer and topographical painter here agree and seem to congratulate each the other on his skill. Fulvio Roiter, in his photographs, pays Canaletto the compliment of drawing attention to the mechanical accuracy of the painter's eye and hand in delineating with a very thin brush outlines of walls, embrasures, roofs, exactly as confirmed by his own lens, whilst Canaletto can be supposed to congratulate Fulvio Roiter and his camera (Venetians loved mechanical aids to painting) on a subtlety of line and gradation of colour which his artist's human eye confirms.

Another aspect of Canaletto has compliments paid to it by the photograph of the Vogalonga (*161*) – the boat parade held annually of recent years, opposite the Ducal Palace. This rivals Canaletto's accuracy in his paintings of gondolas, oars, poles, rowing and punting figures, depicted in gleaming ridges of red, ochre, sepia, green.

There are photographs here of architectural features which Guardi caricatures – almost – in drawings in sepia and in certain paintings. If one tries to think of Guardi as a photographer it will be of one with some very special sort of distorting lens. Looking at the photographs of the Procuratie Vecchie (*41*) and the Palazzo Giustiniani (*82*) one sees how in a Guardi drawing, architectural features of windows, pillars, balustrades, steps, poles, are changed as though to musical phrases spaced and struck rhythmically on an instrument. These sketched strokes spluttered from a quill in sepia ink and smudged in places – rapid, spontaneous and seemingly carefree – add up to pages which look like music of a most lively yet elegant score. The Guardi drawings bring us back to Venice seen as accurately as if it had been photographed.

The photograph of the façade of the Ducal Palace (*19*) puts me in mind of Monet's treatment of palaces along the Grand Canal, his contrasting the cold stone above with the curved brushwork depicting the water, a dark web netting the reflected light of the marble above it.

The camera's eye can produce images complementing those of the painter, but, of course, in the hands of Fulvio Roiter it reveals aspects of Venice unique to photography. The camera fixes moments of vision so fleeting that before we have time to record them they have escaped us. Examples of these are the carving of a lion's head trailing stony ribbons (*141*); the tunnelled darkness of the passage-way leading from the Ponte de lo Spade and the beautiful lettering of that name above the arch (*142*); and the dense, rich, deep-crimson, almost damask texture of one of the walls of the courtyard of the Ducal Palace. The camera can also be a quietly amused observer, as in the photograph of the chalk drawings of gondolas drawn on a wooden door (*140*). With exposures of 1/500 second it freezes the patterns made by fireworks on the night of the Redentore (*174*) with lights falling in bright scratched strokes against spirals of fountaining smoke into a sea of squiggling serpents and horizontal azure dashes. Fulvio Roiter has recaptured modern scenes of regattas, pageants, theatres, dance – painted by Venetians and described by Byron in his letters – within the context of today's tourists. One has the impression of the life of Venetians continuing with little break from the past, yet being swamped by the tourists, the omnivorous devouring present.

The photographs here least characteristic of the photographer are those taken from the air, especially the ones of the Ducal Palace and of sections of the Grand Canal. These may give little scope for his genius yet they give me the kind of satisfaction I get from Giorgio Morandi's still-lifes of bottles and other objects. Just as one can, in the eye of one's mind, take a walk between Morandi's objects, as though along alleyways and little squares of his native Bologna, so, looking at the aerial photograph of St Mark's Square (*38*) I can walk out of the Piazza through the passage which leads past steps going to the Correr Museum, past the Capella San Moisè, across a bridge with, on my left, the ugly modern Bauer-Grünwald Hotel, and then along the wide (for Venice!) fashionable street of shops and tourist agencies, the Calle

Larga 22 Marzo. Looking again at the building-crammed, *calle-* and canal-fissured aerial photographs, I remember those consciously aimless walks I used to take when I first went to Venice as an undergraduate. I see now that to get to the Rialto Bridge from the Piazza I would – very absurdly – walk nearly the whole length of the Grand Canal trying, when forced through narrow passages past the crammed and bulky backs of those palaces which front the canal in marble magnificence – not to lose touch with the canal itself – to retain glimpses of its traffic-hurrying water and, if that proved impossible, at least to hear the honks and shouts of its *autoscafoli* and gondoliers.

The fact that so many buildings and even statues in Venice have splendidly carved fronts, but backs which are only structures improvised to support them, has caused much unfavourable comment, not least from Ruskin. But as the princely artists, composers, poets and theatrical directors who came here have always understood, Venice is nothing if not theatre. It has put on the bravest show of all cities of all time, and in that perhaps lies the secret of its survival. Only Napoleon tried to call her bluff by stealing the bronze horses from the verandah of St Mark's. He fell, they pranced back into place. Venice is like a great flamboyant opera singer who for centuries has been giving her

12

final last performance before total retirement. Occasionally there is a sensational breakdown to prove that this stone flesh is really rotting as when, in 1902, the Campanile (without hurting anyone) collapsed into the Piazza below, sending up a volley of pigeons.

One can think of Venice then as a matter of screens and floats and wings which goes completely dead when the lights (which include the special pointilliste effects of starlight) are not on. Wandering through its mazes away from the magnetic centres of touristic attention, one notes that it has already gone dead in certain areas. When my son and I were there in June, for the first two days it rained. Venice seemed a gloomy deserted stage-set of discoloured dripping cardboard walls – scenery in an unlighted theatre. We walked to a district not far from the Rialto Bridge, which seemed to be falling completely into disrepair. Windows were boarded up, gaps opened onto voids, shutters fell sideways, there were areas of broken glass, flapping rags, sneaky cats, and no-one about. At such moments Venice might be some negative philosophic concept, an abstract colourless thing-in-itself which does not exist until opened up by the perceiving senses of an observer.

But then the sun came out, the lights were switched on, the back-cloth of sky above the roofs and chimneys along the Grand Canal was shown to be blue, faintly tinted with yellows which picked up the colours of the marble on the façades below and were reflected again in the water of the Grand Canal.

If one has been there several times, across intervals of several years, one seems to carry the memory of each visit upon one's body, like stigmata upon the flesh of some silk- or velvet-attired saint in a Tintoretto. The stigmata from my earliest visits were especially evident upon my feet, for playing my game of getting lost in the *calli* and along the canals, I would walk until they bled from the imprint of the incredibly hard pavements of Istrian limestone.

The advantage of getting lost was that one found so much. Every few yards there were surprises, of which many of the photographs in this volume provide evidence. A dark passage-way opens onto the wide brilliantly lit expanse of a square enclosed by houses of different heights with narrow steep shuttered windows in grey peeling walls. At each corner a *calle* leads out of the square. I do not know which to consider the continuation of the one by which I have entered. Nor do I care. On one side of the square there is a shop, with a window full of toys. In the square itself there is a booth where a few vegetables lie on a bench under a striped awning. There is also a marble well-head in the form of the capital of a Corinthian column, the stone polished to shining whiteness on top, scratched and rather dirty below. Choosing at random my way

13

out of the square I go along a *calle* which leads to a bridge over a canal. The tops of the balustrades are polished to a glassy whiteness by the hands and sleeves of generations of passers-by, reminding me of a rocky cave which I once came to in Greece, whose walls were brightened by the fleeces of generations of what I supposed to be Homeric sheep. I walk on. Suddenly the *calle* opens onto what seems a series of stone platforms descending like immense steps to the Grand Canal, with the high brick wall of a church on my right and, beyond it, a smart-looking gallery of modern art. To my left there are flower-stalls and beyond them, just before the Grand Canal, a garden which, as always in Venice, looks out of place and rather shockingly green. And then – for this is where, through losing my way, I have got – there is the modern wooden structure, strutted and steeply arched and looking as though it stands on stilts, of the Accademia Bridge.

Standing on the middle of the bridge and looking up the Grand Canal, I can take in the difference of Venetian from all other architecture. To my left and right, the great palaces rise cliff-like from the water, most of them tall, but a few squat. These façades are of multi-coloured marble slotted with windows, some steeply arched and lance-like, others like greatly enlarged key-holes of treasure chests. The edges of the palace roofs against the sky are serrated, wave-like, as though holding up against the sky a motif repeated from the rippling waves of the canal below. Tall elaborately moulded chimneys stand darkly above the roofs like pennons assaulting the sky. These chimneys remind me of armour and skulls in the dragon-haunted landscapes of Carpaccio. Far below, poles rise from the water. Some poles are black and gold, some white, with diagonal vermilion stripes. They are surmounted by armorial bearings and seem the sparse outer defences of immense massive wet stones at the base of the palaces which reach down into the water, like the immensely strong and ancient roots of some great multi-trunked and branched tree growing in a tropical swamp.

The marble façades of certain elaborate gothic palaces have a quality like wrought Moroccan leather-work, with incised or fret-sawed clover-shapes or geometrical patterns of darker stone inlaid within a base of contrasting colour. Adrian Stokes writes:

> There exists in the Gothic palace windows flanked by porphyry or serpentine disks, a constant communication – and a musical one – between the inside and the outside world, as if flambeaux burnt steadily near the balconies and the palace lay open to the night music of the serenade.

Henry James' heroine Milly in *The Wings of a Dove* subsides almost under this interplay of the inner and the outer Venice, when she enters into temporary possession of a palace on the Grand Canal (it is the Palazzo Barbaro) to receive her guests for the tragedy of her Venetian honeymoon that never takes place:

> Not yet so much as this morning had she felt herself sink into possession; gratefully glad that the warmth of the Southern summer was still in the high florid rooms, palatial chambers where hard cool pavements took reflexions in their life-long polish, and where the sun on the stirred sea-water, flickering up through open windows, played over the painted 'subjects' in the splendid ceilings – medallions of purple and brown, of brave old melancholy colour, medals as of old reddened gold, embossed and beribboned, all toned with time and all flourished and scolloped and gilded about, set in their great moulded and figured concavity (a nest of white cherubs, friendly creatures of the air) and appreciated by the aid of that second tier of smaller lights, straight openings to the front, which did everything, even with the Baedekers and photographs of Milly's party dreadfully meeting the eye, to make the place an apartment of state.

The outside of this palace was doubtless gazed at by the young Ezra Pound when at the beginning of the present century he first went to Venice:

> And the palazzo, baseless, dawn hangs there
> With low mist over the tide-mark;
> And floats there nel tramonte
> With gold mist over the tide-mark.

To savour the real stoniness of Venice, I would wander from the Grand Canal to the Paglia Bridge just beyond the front of the Ducal Palace. Standing on the bridge I would look not upwards at the Bridge of Sighs, but sidelong towards this corner of the Ducal Palace, from which there curves outwards the stone foliage of the vine-tree framing the lurching figure of the drunken Noah. This grouping protrudes from the base of the Ducal Palace almost like a prow. The chiselled whiteness of the salty-looking stone, concentrates for me the idea of the contrasts of stone and water, about which Adrian Stokes in prose and Ezra Pound in poetry have written with brilliance. Here is Pound in the Cantos:

> Venice
> Forest of marble
> Dye pots in the torchlight,
> The flash of wave under prows
> And the silver beaks rising and crossing.
>   Stone trees, white and rose-white in the darkness,
> Cypress there by the towers,
>   Drift under hulls in the night

My wanderings, not just when I was an undergraduate, but throughout the years, brought me always back to St Mark's Square, which has been compared to a ball-room, but which to my mind is more like the central chamber, interior cavity of a body, containing the heart. For St Mark's Basilica truly is the hollow centre of Venice, with its great arched porch, and two attendant porches each side; above the central porch a long gallery with a balustrade, wide enough to contain the four horses looted from Byzantium by the Venetians and later taken to Paris by Napoleon; and behind that a second tier of a great pointed arch and two attendant arches; and, crowning all, the central dome with attendant lesser domes. The panoply of bristling spikes and turrets surmounting the façade with Ruskin's white dome behind it remind me of the spikes on the helmet of Tartar emperors, and give the multi-domed cathedral with the bronze horses standing above the central porch the look of a body armoured, self-protecting, guarding its own interior darkness, a cavernous interior within an outer space – that of the Piazza – filled with loot certainly worth protecting, gold-gleaming mosaic, lamps, candles, columns, vestments, everything in place but different from anything else (each pillar or column a separate piece of plunder from Byzantium), precious stolen objects shrouded in darkness. And the floor of stone slabs in waves, seeming to imitate the waves of the Lagoon outside.

One never forgets in Venice that the city is completely unlike anywhere else. Venice is a marble lung at this end of the Adriatic which breathes in and breathes out – inhales and exhales – each day, according to the tides, the sea. The sea does – or did – take away its ordures and renew it with clean water. The city has no other system of sanitation. The pretence that other cities which have canals – Amsterdam, for example – are like Venice only shows the difference. They merely have canals. To Venice canals are water, air, blood. The harbour has entered into every crevice in the city, become its very existence. Thus transport in Venice means the sea – traditionally the gondola. This introduces into it an element or condition which is like a different dimension of time. To recognize this, one only has to consider, for example, the effect upon New York if all the streets and avenues of Manhattan were excavated and made into canals!

Another result of this induction into the city of the element which was defence for the original settlers, fleeing before Barbarian invaders, is that one never loses awareness, in Venice, of the miraculous. 'Turn but a stone, and start a wing!' Walk here but twenty yards and you are confronted by the miracle that the original settlers, families from the ruinous Roman Empire, built this city amid sands and water, bringing from far away every log from which to make the piles and every stone to place upon them.

The recurrent theme of Venetian art is the miracle of Venice itself. In Tintoretto's great painting at the Accademia, *The Translation of the Body of St Mark*, the moment of the miracle is depicted as that when Venetian envoys went to Alexandria to obtain the saint's body and brought it to Venice. Lightning streaks from the sky and reveals a square which is reminiscent of St Mark's itself. Awed citizens terrified by the fire descending from heaven take flight under arcades at the sides of the square. The most important of the three Venetian envoys who bear the classically modelled beautiful silver-skinned corpse of the saint, is clad in purple velvet. One feels that although God has signed from the sky that he approves the miracle, it is entirely the work of man, the self-made Venetians. The sumptuous attire of the chief envoy affirms that this is the case.

For the miracle of Venice envisioned by Renaissance Venetian art is to have transformed the poverty, the desolation, of these weed-tufted islands into marble, gold, jewels, velvet, silks and dyes. The greater the show put on, the greater the contrast with what went before, and, therefore, the greater the miracle. Every carved pillar looted from Byzantium, every shipful of merchandise traded with the East, is a repetition of the miracle. For this reason when the Venetians paint a beggar, he or she is likely, if a man, to be dressed in velvet, if a woman, to wear pearls and diamonds. For the Venetians, the beggar is a symbol of what Venice has become. The miracle is, of course, religious, because the gods – pagan, or Christian Trinity – sit in their heaven and applaud the battles won, the treaties signed, the wealth obtained by the sumptuously attired Venetians. So much Istrian marble transported, like the marble body of St Mark, to enrich these islands, so much wealth wrung from barren wastes.

How typical of the Venetian attitude that, when questioned by the Inquisitors as to the appropriateness of certain of the stage properties of his painting of the Last Supper, Veronese simply changed the title of this great banquet scene to *The Supper in the House of Levi*.

The ambiguity of the relationship of the miraculous to the religious, on the one hand, and the individualistically human, on the other, sheds a good deal of light on one's own ambiguous feelings towards Venice. The city and its history and achievements almost illustrate the double meaning of the word 'genius' – and no city ever showed greater quantities of this commodity – as meaning that which comes from God, or that which is demonic, comes from Satan. One is reminded of Blake's remark that Milton, in depicting God overthrowing Satan, was of the Devil's party without knowing it. Satan signifies energy, and never was energy more vigorously displayed than in Venice.

17

Of course, the Venice we see is posthumous as regards its own history, its own art, its own genius. Nevertheless the preservation of this miracle becomes a reason for perpetuating it. If Venice sank under the sea the evidence of the aesthetically miraculous would, in great part, have disappeared from the earth. That we should live to see it do so would be a judgement on our unaesthetic world of ugliness. One half believes that the outside world will brace itself to some miracle of its own mechanistic modern ingenuity to save Venice. In the very fragility of this marble magnificence lies its appeal.

STEPHEN SPENDER

18

one   **Genesis: a city rising from the sea**

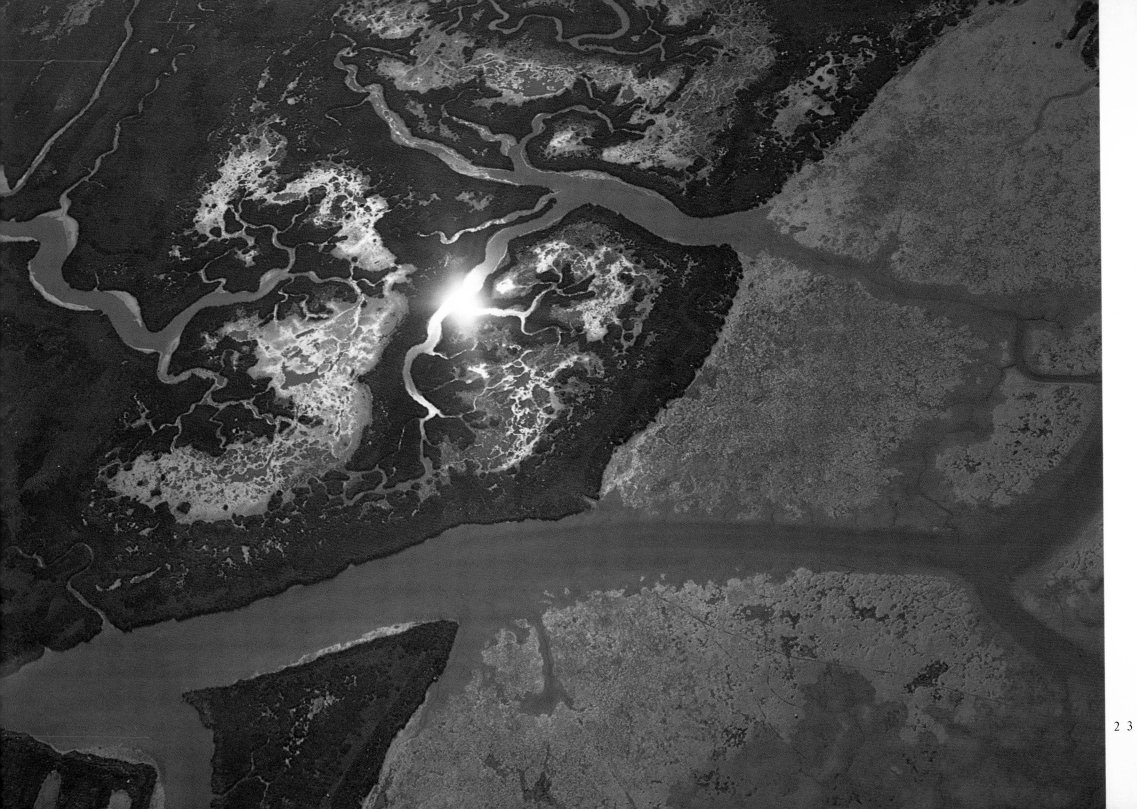

23

12 13

14 15

1

The calm waters of the Adriatic Sea, seen from the shore. Strategically placed at the northern end of the Adriatic, the city and Republic of Venice once dominated and controlled the major trade routes between Europe and the East. It saw the passage of Crusaders sailing to the Holy Land and of ships laden with spices and treasures returning from the East. The tiny Republic's geographical position was to form the basis of its historical power and resulting wealth and splendour, which reached their zenith in the fifteenth century.

2, 3

The fringes of the Adriatic near Venice, where the low-lying plain traversed by important rivers meets the sea, creating a maze of lagoons and islands bordered by muddy shoals; such were the uncertain foundations on which the earliest settlers in this area had to build in the fifth to seventh centuries.

4, 5

In the shallow waters near the shore it was necessary to sink wooden piles (known as *bricole*) into the mud to provide foundations for landing-stages and to indicate channels for safe navigation. This tradition began with the first settlers, who chose this seemingly un-inviting environment in preference to the mainland where they were threatened by the barbarian hordes. Ever since, Venice has retained its close association with and dependence on the sea, an association which gives the city its unique quality.

6–9

Founded in the ninth century, the city itself overlooks the Lagoon; seen from a distance, the buildings seem to rise out of the water – an incomparable view which greets every traveller arriving by sea.

St Mark's Basin leads directly to the heart of the city, where many of the most imposing and exciting buildings are concentrated. The buildings on the left (*7, 9*) stand on the island of San Giorgio; on the right, the dominating feature is the campanile of St Mark's (*15, 38*).

10

The island of San Giorgio, with the late sixteenth-century church of S. Giorgio Maggiore (by Andrea Palladio) and its campanile seen in silhouette. From the earliest times, it was on this island, standing directly opposite the Doge's Palace and the Piazzetta of St Mark's, that ships would tie up.

11
The church of S. Giorgio seen from the Riva degli Schiavoni, to the east of the Doge's Palace. This church is famous for its two major works by Tintoretto – *The Fall of Manna* and *The Last Supper*. Today, the island of San Giorgio is leased as the headquarters of an important cultural and educational organization, the Cini Foundation, which has taken over and restored the former monastery buildings dating from the sixteenth and seventeenth centuries; these buildings contain a magnificent staircase and library by Longhena.

12, 13
The landing-stage for gondolas, close by the Piazzetta of St Mark's, seen at dusk; the outlines of the church of Sta Maria della Salute, standing on the opposite side of the Grand Canal, are softened by the fading light.

14
The island of San Giorgio momentarily bathed in sunlight while the city itself remains in shade; a small lighthouse, one of two built in the nineteenth century, stands at the east entrance to the island's tiny harbour.

15
The imposing city centre, seemingly rising out of the Lagoon, seen from the island of San Giorgio. The buildings shown are: on the left, the sixteenth-century Libreria Vecchia (Old Library) by the Florentine sculptor and architect Jacopo Sansovino; behind it, the 325-ft campanile of St Mark's (the original tower collapsed in 1902 and was rebuilt as an exact replica in the following decade); in the centre, the Piazzetta of St Mark's, with its twin columns, one surmounted by a marble statue of St Theodore (first patron saint of Venice), the other by the symbolic winged lion of St Mark (this is a modern copy; the original is now preserved in the Doge's Palace); in the background, the Clock Tower and part of St Mark's Basilica; and, right, the Doge's Palace.

This is one of the city's most familiar panoramas, much loved by artists who have used it as the subject of engravings and paintings down the centuries.

16
The façade of the Doge's Palace, in the evening light, seen from a fast motor-boat. Such boats, available for hire, are typical of present-day Venice – in contrast to the more leisurely world of the traditional and familiar gondolas plying the city's canals.

two   **The heart of Venice**

29 30 31

43 44

47 48

49 50

17

The centre of Venice as seen from the air reveals a maze of waterways, streets and squares, spreading outwards from the Grand Canal, the city's main artery, which is traversed by the graceful Rialto Bridge, completed in 1592. In this crowded and congested area all manner of activities – commercial, religious, domestic, social – contribute to the daily life of the city.

18, 19

The Doge's (or Ducal) Palace and St Mark's Basilica seen from the air, and the façade of the Palace overlooking St Mark's Canal and the Lagoon. The intricate symmetry of arcades and loggia, and the geometric patterning of the marble facing – the twelfth-century building was altered and enlarged in the fourteenth and fifteenth centuries at the height of the Venetian Republic's prosperity – reveal the Palace as a masterpiece of Venetian Gothic architecture.

To the right of the Palace, a small canal – the Rio di Palazzo – leads to the heart of the city; it is traversed first by the Paglia Bridge; then by the famous Bridge of Sighs leading directly from Palace to prisons; and finally by the Canonica Bridge. The horseshoe-shaped Palace encloses a courtyard, in which can be seen the spires of the Foscari Arch (late fifteenth century), abutting on the Basilica.

20, 21

The Paglia Bridge crowded with visitors; it is so named because boats loaded with straw (*paglia*) used to tie up there. Further up the Rio di Palazzo can be seen the enclosed Bridge of Sighs, built *c.* 1600; it owes its name to its historical associations with prisoners who, after undergoing trial by inquisition in the Doge's Palace, were led across it to prison or execution.

22

A view of the shady Rio di Palazzo and the Bridge of Sighs, seen from the Paglia Bridge; the walls of the 'New' prisons, built in the sixteenth and seventeenth centuries, are on the right.

23

The bases of the twin granite columns in the Piazzetta of St Mark's, with the colonnade of the Doge's Palace beyond. The sculpted reliefs at the foot of each column date from the twelfth century and represent the crafts.

24
Close to the Porta della Carta, leading to the Doge's Palace, and set against the façade of the Basilica of St Mark's, is the fourth-century porphyry group popularly known as 'the Moors'. Legend has it that the figures represent a group of Saracens who set out to steal the treasures of the Basilica and that the sculpture was placed against the wall near the Treasury. In fact, the figures are of tetrarchs at the time of the Roman emperor Diocletian, and were originally brought from Egypt.

25, 26
Marble columns, and a detail of the balustrade, of the first-floor loggias – overlooking the Lagoon and the inner courtyard, respectively – of the Doge's Palace. The capitals here are less ornate than those of the ground-level arcades.

27, 28
Two views of the loggia overlooking the inner courtyard of the Doge's Palace (south and east sides). This courtyard, completed in the sixteenth century, is an outstanding example of Renaissance architecture;

the round arches of the arcade were inserted later, in the early seventeenth century.

29
Inside the loggia, the walls are lined with nineteenth-century busts of Venetian Doges, each wearing the distinctive ducal cap.

30
The statue of Mars by Jacopo Sansovino (1554); with its companion figure of Neptune, it stands at the top of the Scala dei Giganti – the Giants' Stairway – which takes its name from these two over-lifesize statues. This grand staircase, situated in the inner courtyard opposite the main entrance of the Palace, was the place of formal installation for successive Doges, when they were presented with the symbolic cap of office.

31
The Scala d'Oro – Golden Stairway – with the loggia and courtyard below; designed by Sansovino, this beautiful stairway is decorated with stuccos by Alessandro Vittoria. Completed in 1558, the stairway leads to the upper floors of the Palace, including the Doge's private

apartments; the Palace also contains the offices of the former state dignitaries of the Republic, and was a complete and self-contained centre of government, in the tradition of the imperial palaces of ancient Rome, as was the Topkapi Palace in Constantinople (which city was occupied by the Venetians in the thirteenth century, at the time of the Fourth Crusade).

32
Leaving the Grand Council Chamber, the centre of government of the former Venetian Republic; the most spectacular room in the Palace, it measures approximately 175 × 75 ft and has a magnificent unsupported ceiling. Both the walls and ceiling are decorated overall with frescos and paintings by great masters, including Titian, Veronese and Tintoretto.

33
The Sala dell'Anticollegio, anteroom to Sala del Collegio (a grand reception room), looking back into the Sala delle Quattro Porte (Hall of the Four Doors). The decoration of this anteroom includes four

paintings of mythological subjects by Tintoretto (the lower half of one of these, *Mercury and the Three Graces*, is shown).

34
The domes of St Mark's Basilica silhouetted against the setting sun. The plan of the present church, in the form of a Greek cross, is the key to the positioning of the four smaller domes, over the arms of the cross, around the large central dome. The original church, a shrine built in honour of the remains of the saint brought to Venice from Alexandria in the ninth century, was rebuilt and enlarged in the eleventh and twelfth centuries.

35
The famous group of bronze horses which stands above the central doorway of the Basilica is a copy of a Greek original of the third century BC, brought to Venice from Constantinople after the Fourth Crusade (1204). The Roman copy, probably dating from the second century AD, formerly adorned the Hippodrome in Constantinople; in 1797, in the Napoleonic period, the group was removed to France, but was returned to Venice after the signing of the Treaty of Vienna (1815).

36
A glimpse of St Mark's Square from the entrance to the Basilica; on the right we see part of one of the two bronze doors of the central entrance portal.

37
An interior view of St Mark's Basilica, showing some of the gold decoration which gave rise to the description *chiesa d'oro* (golden church); the wealth of the Republic, arising largely from its contacts with the East and the Byzantine tradition, led to the extremely lavish decoration with marble and mosaics which were continuously added to and embellished over a long period. The Basilica, once the chapel of the Doges, is now the city's cathedral – one of the most beautiful of all churches.

38
A view over the Doge's Palace, the Basilica and St Mark's Square, dominated by the simple lines of the campanile towering above the surrounding buildings. The square was once large enough to accom-modate the city's entire population, whenever public ceremonial or festive occasions demanded.

Other notable buildings recognizable in this close-packed area are: (top left) the church of Sta Maria del Giglio, built in the seventeenth century by Sardi, notable for its prominent statuary; (also on the left, just beyond the square) the back of another seventeenth-century church, S. Moisè, notable for its statues by Merengo; (top, to the right of the campanile) the city's principal theatre, La Fenice; and an architectural curiosity (right, background) the ascending spiral of the staircase of the fifteenth-century Palazzo Contarini del Bovolo, a feature that has been likened to a snail-shell.

39, 40
A moment of relaxation – a visitor pauses to reflect on the architectural wonders that surround one when sitting at an open-air café in St Mark's Square; and even an awning temporarily screening the view of the square can provide a point of interest.

41
The Procuratie Vecchie – formerly the homes of the city's principal officials, known as the Procuratori – on the north side of St Mark's

Square; begun in the fifteenth century, they were completed by Sansovino, whose work predominates in this area close to the Doge's Palace.

42
A view across St Mark's Square, from the roof of the Procuratie Vecchie. The buildings opposite, completed by Longhena, were built between 1586 and 1640 and, being more recent, are called the Procuratie Nuove; the narrow west end, or wing, of the square is occupied by the so-called Ala Napoleonica, built by Giuseppe Soli in 1810. The entrance to the Museo Correr, one of the city's important art galleries, is in the arcade, and close by are the Museo del Risorgimento and the Museo Archeologico.

43, 44
Under the Procuratie – open-air cafés. The square was formerly paved with bricks, set in herring-bone pattern; these were replaced in 1723 with paving designed by Andrea Tirali.

45
Inside the 'Old Florian', one of several famous cafés in the Procuratie

buildings, much frequented by visitors to Venice; this is the oldest – it first opened its doors in 1720, when it was owned by Floriano Francesconi, whose name it still bears. The present furniture and decorations date from the nineteenth century.

46
Another famous café in St Mark's Square is Lavena's, which retains an old-world flavour with its graceful crystal chandeliers of Murano glass (made on the island of Murano in the Venetian Lagoon), for which Venice is renowned.

This lavish interior provides a stark contrast with the functional outdoor tables and chairs that first catch the visitor's eye, and are perhaps the more likely choice in fine weather.

47, 48
St Mark's Square is a popular meeting place for tourists and Venetians alike, and like city squares the world over, is frequented by large numbers of pigeons.

49, 50
School groups from Italy and abroad make regular educational visits

to Venice, to receive at first hand an introduction to the city's historic buildings and cultural heritage.

51–53
Rain and the effects of high tides in St Mark's Square. Regular flooding, caused by a seasonal combination of weather conditions and high tides, is a hazard familiar to Venetians; special portable catwalks (*57, 58*) are provided to allow pedestrians to cross the square.

The worst flooding in recent times occurred in 1966, causing serious damage to buildings and art treasures, and giving rise to international concern for the future protection of the city. As a result, the 'Venice in Peril' fund and other organizations were set up to collect urgently needed money for the restoration programme. Teams of specialists equipped with every kind of modern scientific aid have since been working to ensure that no similar tragedy shall occur again.

54, 55
Winter scenes in St Mark's Square – views towards: the Piazzetta; and the Procuratie Vecchie and Ala Napoleonica. Because snowfalls occur outside the tourist season, and then only infrequently, the magical effect produced (*56–60*) is one that visitors rarely see.

86

56–58
Snowy conditions in the Piazzetta and St Mark's Square (with the base of the campanile and part of the Procuratie Nuove); the temporary catwalks for pedestrians are stacked in readiness for the next flooding in the square, which may happen at high tide any time between November and March.

59, 60
Familiar scenes transformed by snow: the island of San Giorgio; and the church of Sta Maria della Salute (near the entrance to the Grand Canal), a magnificent votive church designed by Longhena in 1631 and completed in 1681, dedicated to the Virgin after an epidemic of the plague had ended.

61
The Bocca di Piazza by night. Approaching St Mark's Square from the Calle dell'Ascenzione, through the arcade of the Ala Napoleonica, one has a distant view of the façade of the Basilica, which stands at the opposite end of the now deserted square.

three   **The Grand Canal**
                and other waterways

65 66

71

84 85

89 90

91 92

93

62
A gondolier on the Grand Canal, the city's main artery; the familiar winding course of the canal follows that of an ancient river, which entered the sea at this point on the Adriatic coast.

63
A gondolier relaxes at St Mark's landing-stage; the services of the city's gondoliers are in constant demand, both from Venetians wishing to take a short cut along or across the Grand Canal and from tourists wishing to see the sights in the time-honoured fashion – a leisurely ride using Venice's traditional method of transport.

64
Gondolas tied up to the familiar wooden piles (*bricole*) are part of the everyday scene; the red one in the foreground stands in front of Harry's Bar. The church of Sta Maria della Salute is seen on the opposite bank of the canal.

65
Gondoliers in traditional attire await their next customers; these men and their craft typify the association of Venice with waterways and the sea.

66
A gondolier makes use of his own boat to take a siesta; the gondola, on which he depends for his livelihood, is lovingly cleaned and polished, not just to impress, but out of pride in his job.

67, 68
The *fondamente* – streets on either side of canals – often serve as mooring places for gondolas when they are not in use, especially after the busy tourist season is over.

69
An aerial view of the Dogana da Mar – the customs building, standing at the southern entrance to the Grand Canal; behind it we see the church of Sta Maria della Salute, and between them the Patriarchal Seminary (by tradition, the Archbishop of Venice is known as the Patriarch).

70
A view towards Longhena's baroque masterpiece, Sta Maria della Salute, from the opposite bank of the Grand Canal.

71
The Palazzo Dario, overlooking the canal; this elegant building, dating from the late fifteenth century, reflects the transition to the Renaissance style, and is notable for the distinctive sculpted roundels which decorate the façade.

72
The Grand Canal, near the Accademia Bridge; the bridge, one of only three that span the Canal, was built in 1932. It takes its name from the Accademia di Belle Arti, which includes Venice's principal art gallery, the Gallerie dell'Accademia, with its comprehensive range of works by the great Venetian masters.

73
Crossing the Accademia Bridge; owing to lack of funds at the time of its construction, a timber bridge resulted rather than a more substantial one in stone.

74, 75
Outside the Accademia di Belle Arti; the Academy occupies the fifteenth-century buildings of the former school and church of Sta Maria della Carità and the adjacent monastery of the Lateran Canons by Palladio (1560). The Academy and the now separate art galleries, which contain one of the most important collections in Italy, were transferred here in 1807.

76, 77
Further on, also on the left bank of the Grand Canal, stands the Ca' Rezzonico, an important palazzo which is now a museum of eighteenth-century art and culture. The building itself is an outstanding example of Venetian baroque; designed by Longhena in the second half of the seventeenth century and completed in the mid-eighteenth by Giorgio Massari, it features ceiling decorations by G. B. Tiepolo and others.

78
One of the galleries of the Ca' Rezzonico, with an important series of paintings by Pietro Longhi of eighteenth-century life and manners.

The museum also includes sculptures, period rooms displaying original furniture, a reconstruction of an old pharmacy, marionette theatres and costumes.

79, 80
The formal symmetry of the façade of the Ca' Rezzonico seen across the Grand Canal; and a reminder of the continuing importance of the canal as the city's main line of communication for transporting goods. Part of the Palazzo Giustiniani (*81*) is seen on the extreme right.

81
The façade of the Palazzo Giustiniani, on the left bank of the Grand Canal near the Accademia; this is an important example of the Venetian Gothic style, dating from the fifteenth century. Here, Richard Wagner composed Act II of his opera *Tristan and Isolde,* while living in Venice in 1858–9.

82
The adjacent Palazzi – Giustiniani and Foscari – overlooking the Grand Canal, are an imposing reminder of the elegance and splendour of Venetian Gothic architecture. The Doge Foscari, who was deposed,

died in his palace in 1457 from, it is said, a broken heart. Today, the building is the home of the University Institute of Economics and Commerce.

83
The view looking back towards the Palazzo Foscari (left) after negotiating a sharp bend in the Grand Canal; boats of all shapes and sizes are used as the most convenient means of transport.

84, 85
The wares of two specialist shops near the church of S. Tomà: woodcarving is a traditional craft in Venice, and antique dealers are an important element in the commercial life of a city with a long cultural history and a wealth of art treasures from the East as well as from Europe.

86
An aerial view of the Rialto Bridge and its surroundings. This elegant bridge by Antonio da Ponte, with a single span of 90 ft, was completed in 1592. The square building to the left of the bridge, the Fondaco dei Tedeschi, built in the early part of the sixteenth century as a warehouse

for German merchants, now houses the main post office. The white building to the right of the bridge is the Palazzo dei Camerlenghi (*87*) completed in 1528; it was formerly the official seat of the three Camerlenghi, officials appointed to run the state Treasury.

Overlooking the canal, on the right, is the arcaded façade of the Fabbriche Nuove di Rialto, designed by Sansovino; this was built in the second half of the sixteenth century as the headquarters of the magistracy responsible for trade.

87
The single span of the Rialto Bridge provides ample clearance for boats using the Grand Canal; on the right is the Palazzo dei Camerlenghi.

88
The Grand Canal, looking north-east from the Rialto Bridge; at this point the canal makes a sharp turn to the left. The third building from the left, the Ca' da Mosto, dates from the thirteenth century; this palazzo, built for a famous family of seafarers, is one of the oldest surviving buildings overlooking the canal, retaining some elements showing Byzantine influence. It features an open loggia, reflecting the

sense of security, unusual in medieval times, felt by the original owners. Later, from the fifteenth to the seventeenth century, the building became famous as a hotel – the Albergo del Leon Bianco (the White Lion) – which was patronized by visiting dignitaries and by royalty.

89, 90
The Ca' d'Oro ('golden house'), on the right bank of the Grand Canal, is a masterpiece of the ornate late Venetian Gothic style; it was begun *c*. 1421 and completed in 1440. The description 'golden' refers to the gilding of the ornamental features of the façade in its original state. The building is now a museum, open to the public, with an important collection of paintings (including works by Carpaccio, Mantegna, Titian and Guardi), as well as sculptures and tapestries.

91, 92
The Ca' Mocenigo is situated only a short distance from the Palazzo Foscari (*82, 83*), but on the opposite side of the Grand Canal. This is a typical palazzo in the eighteenth-century style, and we see here two aspects of the sumptuous decoration of the Red Salon. The magnificent

chandelier is probably by the workshop of Giuseppe Brati – a master glass-maker of Murano – and is in the so-called 'ciocca' style (literally, 'bunch of flowers'); above it is a ceiling fresco by J. Guarana, executed in 1767, showing the *Apotheosis of the Mocenigo Family*. The rich red of the draperies enhances the brilliance of the gilding on picture frames and accompanying carved wooden putti and allegorical figures. These are attributed to the workshop of the sculptor A. Contarini.

93

The façade of the Palazzo Sagredo, a late fourteenth-century structure which retains Byzantine features of an earlier building on the site; there are many buildings of historic and architectural interest to be found overlooking the numerous *rios*, or small canals, leading off the Grand Canal.

94

Part of the façade of a Gothic palazzo bathed in the warm glow of the sun's rays as they penetrate the narrow confines of a side-canal on the right bank of the Grand Canal, near the Teatro Maliban.

95, 96

Motor-boats and barges ply the Grand Canal in all weathers. The motor-boats, known as *peote*, are a characteristic feature of everyday activity on the Lagoon and canals; the barges, laden with assorted produce according to the season, are making their way to the city's main fruit and vegetable market (*143, 144*), centrally situated near the Rialto Bridge.

97

A boat crosses the deep water channel on the north-east side of the city, making for the island of Murano. Behind it stands the imposing bulk of the eighteenth-century church of the Gesuiti, the plain exterior of which belies the richness of its interior decoration; in this church one can see an important work by Titian, *The Martyrdom of St Lawrence* (1557). The Donà Bridge carrying the Fondamente Nuove (*155*) crosses the entrance to the Rio dei Gesuiti, a canal leading back to the Grand Canal; in the background, the tower of the church of the Santi Apostoli dominates the skyline, and on the left stands the Palazzo Donà delle Rose.

four   **Byways, bridges and boats**

98

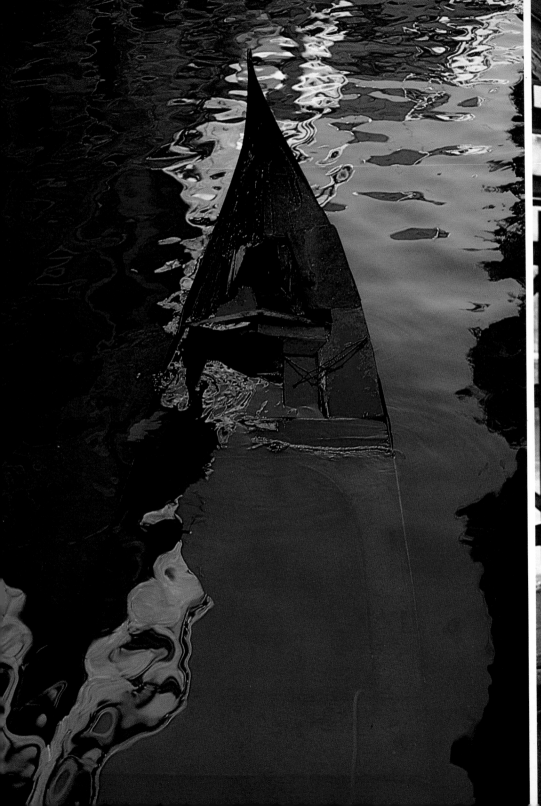

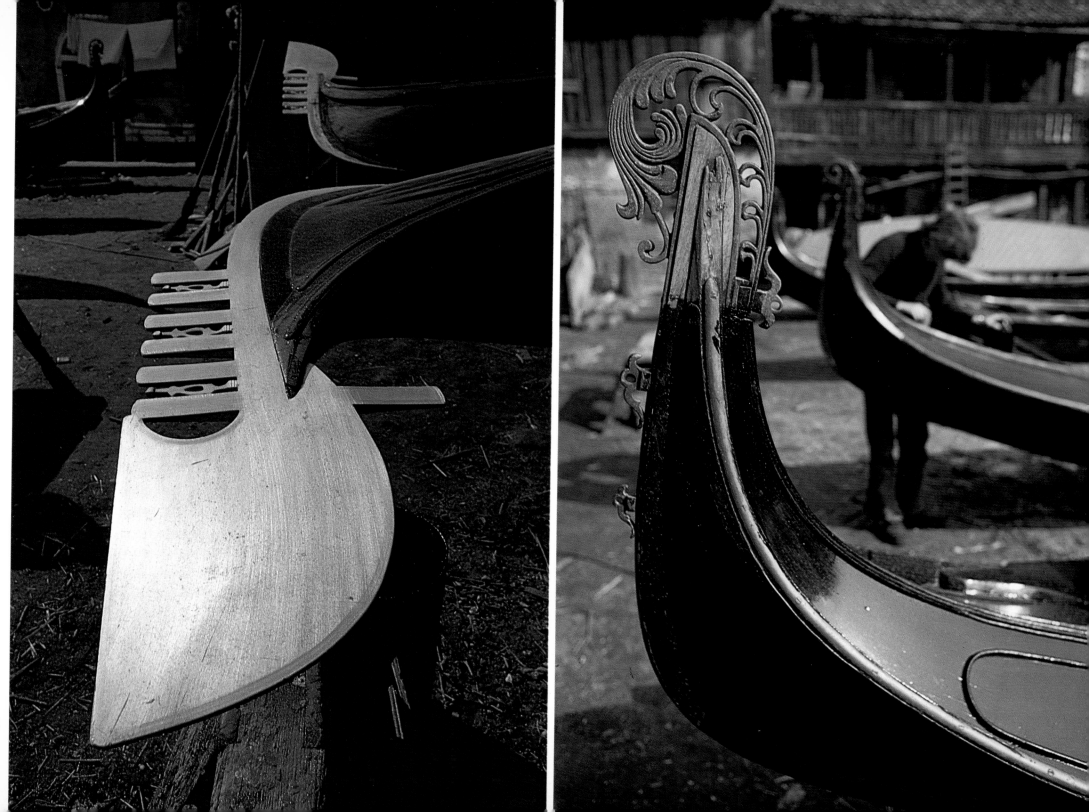

109 110

113 114

PAROCHIA
S: ALVISE
VULGO S. LUDOVICO

SOTOPORTEGO
DE GHETO NOVO.

PONTE DE GHETO
NOVISSIMO

135 136

98
The true character of Venice can only be fully understood and appreciated by viewing the city from the canals, whose narrow confines provide contrasts of light and shade, changing constantly with the changing angle and direction of the sun as the day progresses.

99–104
The building and repairing of gondolas is carried out in boatyards, known as *squeri*; notable examples of such yards are located near the church of S. Trovaso (on the Rio di S. Trovaso, off the Grand Canal) and near S. Pietro di Castello (on the eastern edge of the city).

The shape and form of the gondola that is so familiar today dates from 1562, when the Senate decreed that the boats should all be painted black, but the design is adapted from a very ancient type of craft. The earliest surviving documentary reference dates from 1094, but the design was centuries old even at that time. The standard dimensions of the gondola are 11 metres (about 36 ft) long, and 1·20 metres (about 4 ft) wide; the method of construction has changed little down the centuries. The *squero* itself may have a dilapidated look, but the product of the loving care and attention bestowed on each gondola is a boat in which both maker and owner can justly take pride.

As well as being elegant, the gondola is extremely practical. The heavy metal decorative element – often shaped like a halberd – counterbalances the weight of the gondolier at the stern, and the whole design is one which permits ease of handling and manoeuvrability with the least effort.

105
The traditional skills of the gondolier are learned by Venetian boys at an early age. Here, the Scuola Vecchia della Misericordia provides the background to a scene on the Canale della Misericordia.

106
The gondola also has a vital part to play on important family occasions such as weddings.

107
A floral tribute lying outside on the *fondamenta* by the Rio dei Mendicanti near the principal municipal hospital; a funeral cortège will shortly depart for the nearby island of San Michele which serves as the city cemetery.

108
A funerary wreath being carried across the Campo SS. Giovanni e Paolo; the impressive equestrian statue of Bartolommeo Colleoni, modelled by Verrocchio in the fifteenth century, dominates the background.

109, 110
Special motor-boats are used at funerals for the deceased's final journey by water, before the interment ceremony on the island of San Michele.

111, 112
The church of Sta Maria Formosa, in the heart of the city, is surrounded by a spacious square (*campo*); like many such open spaces, this one is irregular in outline. Open-air stalls, selling all kinds of produce, are a typical feature of the *campi*.

The church itself, largely of the late fifteenth century, has a baroque campanile, added in 1611; the main church fabric was completed in 1492, having been rebuilt by Mauro Coducci, retaining the original ground-plan of the previous church (probably eleventh century). The altarpiece is *Saint Barbara*, an important work by Palma the Elder (1480–1528).

113, 114
A short distance from the Campo Sta Maria Formosa, near the Ospedaletto (almshouse), one encounters in the quiet backwaters evidence of neglect and decay which threatens the very existence of less important buildings; but even here there are still minor architectural gems to be admired.

115–118
Some of the many bridges spanning the canals of Venice – there are some four hundred in all, and the variety is endless.

119, 120
The narrow streets (*calle*) of Venice are often so narrow that it is difficult even for two pedestrians to pass.

121–123
The Arsenal, founded in 1104 and rebuilt in the fifteenth-sixteenth centuries, remains as a symbol of the former Venetian Republic's

power and influence abroad and of its maritime power. This monumental complex, where once some 16,000 people were employed, is on the eastern outskirts of the city; in his *Divine Comedy* – in Canto XX of the Inferno – Dante refers to the Arsenal, the only major historic building in Venice to be mentioned in that great work.

The guardian figures by the gateway – only one being visible here – are war booty: the seated lion shown was taken from the Avenue of Lions on the island of Delos to commemorate the capture of the island of Corfu in the eighteenth century; it dates from the sixth century BC (the head is not original).

124–126
For centuries Venice has had its Jewish community; they originally occupied the island known as La Giudecca, to the south of the city. It was their occupancy, from 1516, of a district in the northern part of the city where there had formerly been a cannon-foundry, that gave rise to the term 'ghetto' (from *getto*, cast), later applied generally to the old Jewish quarters in European cities. In the seventeenth century, there was a Jewish population of about 5,000.

127
For the pedestrian there are many steps and stairs to be negotiated when crossing the numerous bridges which span the canals; the very nature of the narrow streets and bridges permits, even in the twentieth century, an atmosphere of quiet dignity and calm not often encountered in other cities.

128
Staircase in the former Palazzo Centani, near the Rio di S. Tomà on the left bank of the Grand Canal. The famous Italian dramatist Carlo Goldoni was born here in 1707; the house's association with the theatre continues today since it is used as the headquarters of the Istituto di Studi Teatrali.

129, 130
Curious survivals of thirteenth-century sculptures are to be seen in the Campo dei Mori, by the church of the Madonna dell'Orto on the north-east side of the city. Popular tradition has it the three figures (only two are shown) represent Arabian merchants who came to live in Venice in 1112 and installed themselves here in this square – hence the name meaning 'of the Moors'. They were brothers, named Rioba,

Sandi and Alfani, who assumed the surname Mastelli. The figure at the corner (*130*) is popularly known as 'Signor Antonio Rioba', a familiar name in Venetian legend and one used by many writers of satirical pieces.

The painter Tintoretto lived in a house in this square.

131

The church and convent of the Frari, seen from the north-east. This Franciscan foundation, in Venetian Gothic style, was completed in the fifteenth century. Located in the heart of the city, the church is outstanding both architecturally and on account of the famous paintings it contains, including Titian's *Pesaro Madonna* and *Assumption*, and Giovanni Bellini's triptych, *Madonna and Child with Saints*.

The adjacent monastery building now houses the State Archives, one of the richest and most important collections in Europe; the white building in the background is the Scuola di S. Rocco, a sixteenth-century building famous for its collection of large-scale paintings by Tintoretto, including a huge *Crucifixion* and *The Agony in the Garden*. The painter spent a total of eighteen years on the fifty-six paintings he executed for the Scuola.

180

132

In the cloister of the Frari church are several large sculptures, including *Tobias and the Angel* by Francesco Penso; this work dates from the beginning of the eighteenth century. The church itself contains another work by Penso – the reliquary – which can be seen by visitors in the sacristy.

133

The imposing Renaissance entrance to the former Scuola di S. Marco, now a hospital. This was one of six brotherhoods known as the 'Scuole grandi', whose well-to-do members could collectively patronize the greatest artists in competition with the aristocracy; the Scuola di S. Rocco (*131*) was another of these bodies.

134

Votive candles give a warm glow in the dim interior of the church of SS. Giovanni e Paolo. This important church, built in the fourteenth and fifteenth centuries by Dominican friars, stands adjacent to the Scuola di S. Marco (*133*). It contains the tombs of some of the Venetian Doges, as well as important paintings by such artists as Giovanni Bellini, Lorenzo Lotto and Paolo Veronese.

135, 136
Two views of Venice's narrow streets – here there is no concession to old age or infirmity when it comes to negotiating the numerous bridges and flights of steps which are an inevitable feature of everyday life in the city.

137
A group of boys in the Campo Francesco Morosini, by the church of S. Stefano. The open spaces of the *campi* are favourite play areas for children; here we see them gathered around a typical feature of the *campi* – one of the old wells, now closed off, which were the only source of fresh water until a modern piped supply was provided.

138
The appearance of the Campo Francesco Morosini is transformed in warm weather by the outdoor tables of the cafés.

139, 140
The traffic-free streets provide a safe place for children to play; a child's bicycle is the only kind seen in Venice – there are too many obstacles for the bicycle to be a practical means of transport.

141
Figures and heads of lions are encountered everywhere, being the symbol of the evangelist who became the city's patron saint in the ninth century. This head gazes out from the Fondaco dei Tedeschi (*86*), now the main post office, by the Rialto Bridge.

142
The enclosed atmosphere of the narrow streets is here accentuated by having to pass through a tunnel after crossing one of the canal bridges.

143, 144
Scenes in the Rialto market: two women prepare for the day's trading by setting up their vegetable and flower stalls.

The islands along the north coast of the Adriatic are very fertile and suitable for cultivation; the arrival of boats laden with produce (*80, 95*) is in itself a picturesque sight.

145
The parapet of a bridge near the church of Angelo Raffaele (the Angel Raphael), in the western quarter, provides a sunny resting place for one of the city's many cats.

146
A young girl, intent on her errand, turns a corner near the church of Angelo Raffaele; this is the twentieth-century equivalent of the type of scene captured in the work of Francesco Guardi (1712–93). The artist lived in this parish, and the church contains a series of paintings by him (and perhaps also his elder brother Gian Antonio), depicting the story of Tobias and the Angel.

147
A view, looking south-east across the Giudecca Canal, of the church of Il Redentore (the Redeemer) by Andrea Palladio; it was built as a votive offering after an outbreak of the plague in 1576 had ended.

148
Abandoned warehouses of the 1880s, at the eastern end of the island of La Giudecca, stand as a memorial to earlier, unsuccessful, attempts to bring industry to this area.

149, 150
A ship moored in the Giudecca Canal, opposite the eighteenth-century church of the Gesuati; the church, built by Giorgio Massari, contains

182

ceiling paintings by G. B. Tiepolo. This waterway is used by passenger ships, while merchant vessels use a deep-water channel to the mainland port of Marghera.

151
Fisherman at work on their nets on one of the canals of La Giudecca.

152
A ship's mooring ropes frame the church of the Gesuati (*150*) and the buildings along the city's south waterfront, seen across the Giudecca Canal.

153, 154
In the Lagoon, safe navigation by night or in foggy conditions depends on the warning lights, mounted on wooden piles (*bricole*).

155
The Fondamente Nuove run along the north-east waterfront, opposite the island of San Michele. Here we see the steps of the Donà Bridge, adjacent to the Palazzo Donà delle Rose and close to the church of the Gesuiti (*97*). The apse of the church can be seen on the right.

five   **Carnivals, regattas and festivals**

180 181

156–160

Venice has a long carnival tradition, and the masks and costumes seen here reflect something of the sense of history which becomes a reality in the annual events during the pre-Lenten period.

In the eighteenth century, these occasions were an excuse for licentious frolics on a grand scale; today, the tradition lives on, even if only a shadow of the celebrations of past centuries.

161, 162

A recent addition to the city's festive events is the 'Vogalonga', when all kinds of rowing boats – from gondolas to small dinghies – take part in a mass procession on the canal in front of the Doge's Palace. By comparison with other events, this is more a case of general participation than of a spectator-sport.

163–169

The annual Regatta of the Maritime Republics is held on the first Sunday in September, with crews from each of the four former republics – Genoa, Amalfi, Pisa and Venice – taking part in rotation in a traditional pageant in full costume. The costumes of the participants are a colourful reminder of the glory and power of a bygone age.

170, 171

The boats used for the annual Regatta are decked out in traditional style, and the oarsmen dressed in period costume of the fifteenth century. The ceremonial boats, known as *bissone*, are crewed by teams of professional gondoliers hired for the occasion.

172, 173

On the occasion of the annual Regatta, the Grand Canal is transformed by the large number of competing boats; here we see the start of the race and the finishing line, marked by a special pavilion on barges moored between the Palazzo Foscari and the Palazzo Balbi.

This recreation of the centuries-old pageantry, which brings to life scenes familiar from the paintings of Guardi and Canaletto, is a time of great excitement for participants and spectators alike.

174, 175

The Lagoon transformed at night by the brilliant effects of a firework display. Each year in mid-July, the Venetians celebrate the local festival of Il Redentore (the Redeemer); this festival commemorates one of the two occasions in the sixteenth and seventeenth centuries when outbreaks of the plague threatened the city's population. The eventual deliverance of the people, attributed to divine intervention, gave rise to the building of two important churches – Sta Maria della Salute (*60*) and Il Redentore (*147*) – as votive offerings.

The warm summer evening brings forth a host of brightly lit boats, and the occasion – always held at the weekend – is marked by a night-long vigil on the Lagoon, ending only at daybreak on Sunday.

176, 177
La Fenice, Venice's most important theatre, retains an eighteenth-century elegance that is rivalled by very few European theatres. Designed by Antonio Selva, and restored (after a fire in 1836) by the Meduna brothers, this theatre was one of the last important buildings to be completed before the fall of the Venetian Republic; it was inaugurated on 17 May 1792.

178–182
In 1975 the city of Venice witnessed a festival of international ballet – 'Danza '75' – in which many famous companies from all over the world participated. These included the dancers of the Martha Graham company, Béjart's 20th Century Ballet, the Ballet Roland Petit, the Ballet Rambert, the Hamburg company and that of La Scala, Milan.

210

Postscript

It is not easy to re-discover one's own city, photographing it for the third time in twenty years: indeed it is an almost impossible task. My two earlier series of photographic impressions were published in 1954 and 1973.

These two series were almost entirely based on the use of black and white, while the present book represents a truly adventurous approach to colour, spread over a period of two years and requiring a preparation as long and tiring as the one I went through for my book on Brazil; in Venice I experienced the added difficulty of having to observe and re-live the city's reality day after day, with the risk of 'not seeing', or worse, of 'seeing' it badly, whereas in Brazil everything was new and stimulating, appealing to one's sense of the exotic. One thing was immediately clear to me: I had to forget black and white and concentrate on colour alone; in other words, I had to 'think' and 'see' only in terms of Kodachrome. If you consider black and white as a line, colour is a line plus volume. I knew the technique I had learned in my many years' experience of working in black and white would save me from dangerous pitfalls, since on a purely aesthetic level there is no incompatibility between the two ways of exploring reality. But researching must abut on total devotion and on what a photographer should be primarily endowed with, that is the ability of 'seeing' what other people merely 'glance at', in order to make them 'see' beyond the obvious. The great power of suggestion that photography possesses derives from this quality of other people being obliged to see, that is to come to know, places or people by means of captured images.

Personally, I always feel as if I am being subjected to some kind of test, every reportage or book assignment being a kind of examination exercise. I am always mentally photographing something – when speaking, travelling or just sitting quietly. Being a photographer is not a profession, it is a way of life. The choice of the format of the book is not casual or irrelevant; the page size represents an enlargement in direct proportion to the standard frame size of 24 × 36 mm and, given the fact that double pages in an upright format would produce undesirable visual breaks, my choice was logical.

As to technical notes, they are unnecessary here, since I have never resorted to tricks or filters of any kind, even for those photographs which may seem at first to be the result of some strange alchemy. In this case I used, over and over again, the Leica R3, whose new Summicron 50 lens gives extraordinarily good results; I also made great use of the Summilux 55 lens on a Leica M4-2, as well as a Summicron 90. Only for the first and last illustrations in the book did I use the Telyt 560 lens.   Fulvio Roiter

212

Chronology: some important dates

639   Foundation of Torcello cathedral, after the inhabitants of the mainland town of Altino flee to the safety of this island just off the Adriatic coast.

727   Election of the first Doge.

774   Venice besieged by the Franks.

814   The Rivo Alto (modern Rialto) becomes the centre of government and of the city's commercial life. The first shrine is built to house the remains of St Mark, after they have been brought to Venice from Alexandria.

976   A serious fire destroys part of the original St Mark's and some three hundred houses nearby.

1001   Meeting of the Emperor Otto III and Doge Orseolo in Venice.

1003   Work on the construction of the present Basilica of St Mark's begins.

1063   The Doge Contarini begins a new programme of work on the Basilica, which is reopened for worship in 1093.

1124   Venice conquers Tyre.

1192   The Fourth Crusade begins.

1204   Constantinople is captured at the end of the Fourth Crusade, and a Latin Empire established. Many important art treasures, among them the Bronze Horses of St Mark's, are brought to Venice from the East.

1257   Victory of the Venetian fleet over the Genoese gives Venice control of

213

trade with the East – a key development in the Republic's rise to commercial supremacy.

c. 1290 Birth of the first of the great Venetian painters – Paolo Veneziano (died *c.* 1362).

1297 The process of electing the Doges, formerly democratic, is replaced by an oligarchic system, with eligibility for the highest office being restricted to a small number of noble families.

c. 1300 The beginning of the period of architecture in the Venetian Gothic style; this style will predominate for a century and a half.

1340 The building of the Doge's Palace is begun. The Republic embarks on a programme of expansion on the mainland of Italy.

c. 1420 The building of the Ca' d'Oro begins (completed *c.* 1440); today this outstanding palace houses the Galleria Giorgio Franchetti.

1423 The Doge Francesco Foscari embarks on a new phase of expansionism.

1425 The artist Paolo Uccello is brought to Venice to restore the mosaics of St Mark's Basilica.

c. 1430 Jacopo Bellini active in Venice; the earliest paintings by his son, Giovanni, date from *c.* 1450.

1452 Building of the Ca' Foscari begun by the Doge Francesco Foscari; this palace is now used by the University of Venice.

1453 Constantinople falls to the Turks.

c. 1460 The beginning of the period of architecture in the Renaissance style, replacing Venetian Gothic.

1492 The church of Sta Maria Formosa, the masterpiece of Mauro Codussi, is begun.

1529 The arrival in Venice of the architect and planner, Jacopo Sansovino. As official architect to the Republic, he was to be the inspiration and driving force behind a major revival of building activity in the city.

1537 The Libreria Vecchia, designed by Sansovino, is begun.

1555 Andrea Palladio, the greatest architect of the sixteenth century, arrives in Venice.

1557 The Scala d'Oro is built inside the Doge's Palace as the ceremonial entrance to the Collegio and Senate chambers.

1566 The church of S. Giorgio Maggiore is begun by Palladio.

1572 The Venetian fleet takes part in the vital battle of Lepanto, in which the Turks are defeated.

1574 Fire seriously damages the Doge's Palace; in subsequent years much rebuilding and redecoration (by Venetian masters including Tintoretto and Veronese) is undertaken. Tintoretto's major works in the Scuola Grande di S. Rocco also date from this period.

214

1630   After an epidemic of the plague, the architect Baldassare Longhena is commissioned to design a votive church – Sta Maria della Salute – one of the city's major buildings, completed in 1681.

c. 1650   The baroque style begins to make its impact in Venice, notably in the work of Longhena; his two secular masterpieces are the Ca' Rezzonico (begun 1667) and the Ca' Pesaro (begun 1679), overlooking the Grand Canal.

1700   The eighteenth century sees the upsurge of Venetian carnivals and festivities – a period captured in the numerous landscapes of Canaletto (1697–1768) and Guardi (1712–93).

1744   The church of Sta Maria della Pietà begun by Giorgio Massari; this church, completed in 1760, contains an outstanding ceiling fresco – *The Triumph of the Virgin* (1754) – by G. B. Tiepolo.

c. 1750   The beginning of the age of Enlightenment, marked by rationalist philosophy and, in the last quarter of the century, by Neo-Classical architecture.

1792   The opening of the Teatro la Fenice, the city's principal theatre, designed by Antonio Selva.

1797   Abdication of the last Doge and loss of Venice's independence; a period of Austrian rule ensues.

1805   Venice becomes part of Napoleon's *Regno Italico* (until 1815); many reforms instituted and new buildings erected.

1866   Venice annexed to the new Kingdom of Italy.